DESIGNS ON YOUR HOME

For my mother Barbara, whose constant interest in the world of art and design has opened a doorway for me.

DESIGNS ON YOUR
HOME

DAGNY DUCKETT
Photography by Spike Powell

UNWIN

HYMAN

London · Sydney · Wellington

First published in Great Britain by Unwin Hyman,
an imprint of Unwin Hyman Limited.

© Dagny Duckett 1988
Photographs © Spike Powell 1988
Designed by John Grain
Typeset by Nene Phototypesetters Ltd
Printed and bound in Portugal by
Printer Portuguesa, Sintra

UNWIN HYMAN LIMITED
15–17 Broadwick Street, London W1V 1FP

Allen & Unwin Australia Pty Ltd
8 Napier Street, North Sydney, NSW 2060, Australia

Allen & Unwin with the Port Nicholson Press
60 Cambridge Terrace, Wellington, New Zealand

British Library Cataloguing in Publication Data

Duckett, Dagny
    Designs on your home.
    1. Interior decoration
    I. Title
    747   NK2110
ISBN 0–04–440137–X

CONTENTS

INTRODUCTION

PREVIOUS PAGE: With a little imagination, you can create the illusion of space and sunshine with a verandah. The small peacock eye pattern in the cushions on these chairs helps to reinforce an old colonial image of basketwork chairs, hanging plants and bamboo blinds.

When you walk into a room for the first time, a dark room, poorly decorated and cramped for space, it may take a certain amount of imagination for you to transform that room mentally into one you would rather see in its place. You have to look beyond the peeling wallpaper and the shabby paintwork to assess the room for its true qualities: the amount of light it receives during the day, or its length (which may be perfect for the piece of oversized furniture that you already own), for example.

When trying to assess a room or house, practise a 'white washing' method – imagine that all the walls *are* white. Look at the proportions of the room, the size of the windows and the aspect of the room (whether it faces north or south) rather than at the unmade bed or garish wallpaper! We are often put off by the decoration of the property and at the same time so often misled by a well decorated house. Many beautiful houses or flats are passed by because they are depressingly and badly decorated.

Each room has a character of its own, so allow yourself to find that character by looking beyond the immediate decor and imagining how your belongings and colour schemes could transform that room. Start with a piece of furniture that you already own such as a large sofa (which may need a room with a long wall or a room with grand proportions) or a pretty bed-head (perhaps its Victorian lines are echoed in the cornice work in the room), a broken but elegant armchair (which would fit perfectly in that niche by the fireplace) and so on.

It is impossible to picture the final result when redecorating, as the changes are often dramatic although nearly always pleasing. Take one step at a time, and you'll be surprised at how naturally the colour schemes seem to pull together and how often a perfect piece of furniture appears in a junk shop. Another plate or matching cushion may turn up in an antique market or perhaps will be given to you as a birthday present. Whether it takes you a matter of weeks, months or years makes very little difference. Once you start noticing your surroundings and begin to enjoy decorating your home, the whole process takes on an element of fun and pleasure.

Don't be afraid of colour, as very few colours 'clash' in the old sense of the word. After the fifties when new materials were used in furniture production and set ideas changed dramatically, the psychedelic sixties introduced brilliant orange and purple furniture to the general public. Recent designs have positively broken all barriers with traditional furnishings. There are no rules, because taste *is* so individual and today individuality is the key to success in interior design.

Allow your sense of style to dictate what you would like to live with. Don't be put off your stride by magazines with seemingly 'perfect' colour schemes. Most people have a natural sense of colour co-ordination, so use other people's ideas in conjunction with your own to create new schemes.

Very few ideas are totally original, since interiors of houses have been decorated for thousands of years. Every colour of the rainbow has probably been used at some time or another. It is your combination of colours and your possessions that make your house attractive and unique.

The feeling of pleasure and welcome you receive when you walk into a room which you have designed or decorated is parallel to none. Creativity is important to all of us and you needn't be able to paint beautifully or able to build furniture to achieve that feeling. Just designing or putting together a room you love could start a spark of interest in the whole business.

Apart from the pleasure you may get when redesigning your home, the financial gains to be made are enormous. A well decorated property definitely has a better chance of being sold than one which is poorly or shabbily decorated, even though the transformation could be achieved with just a few coats of paint. There are times of course, when it will take a lot more work than a couple of coats of paint but the work is nearly always justified as the value of your house should rise with each improvement you make to it.

Whether the final image you hope to achieve is modern, hi-tech or cottage-like, you may need to look at your furniture and decide on a suitable backdrop or stage to show off your belongings.

Change the house you live in or are about to live in to one in which you will feel more comfortable, enjoy walking into and, most of all, into a house you feel is your home.

CHAPTER 1

DRAMATIC CHANGES

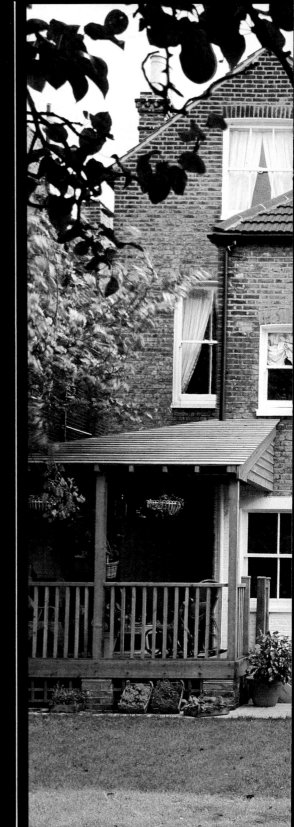

PREVIOUS PAGE AND RIGHT: One of the greatest face lifts you can give the exterior of your property is a coat of white paint. Although little of the actual brickwork has been altered, the contrasting white woodwork makes the house overleaf appear scrubbed clean. The area to the left of the house used to be very dark, so little grew there. A wooden verandah was the ideal solution, with doors from the children's playroom opening out onto it allowing them to play outside during bad weather. The old, brick extension was removed and replaced with the glass conservatory, which reinforced the feeling of light and space. The final effect of the conservatory and verandah balances the house.

If you plan enormous changes to your home, you will need to spend some time in each room with a sketch of the projected result or a clear image of how the changes will affect the room as the finished look can be incredibly different to the original plan.

It is sometimes rather a shock to see the new space that is created when a wall is removed between two rooms. The football stadium that you had imagined might appear may not present itself, or the room may suddenly seem far too big, one end unconnected to the other, so that the one large room you had hoped for is still not achieved. There are ways to get around both of these problems without losing the character of the rooms. The chapter on coping with large and small rooms deals with these problems in detail.

You may find that changes are too costly to be worthwhile to the layout of the property. However, the changes that ensue when you have just *one* wall removed can be staggering – the extra space you've created can completely alter the feeling of the house.

The rooms we choose as bedrooms, kitchens or living rooms are usually defined as such by their shape, size or position in the house. If we can change some of these requirements, then it may be possible to recreate these rooms for other purposes.

The fixed appearance of a kitchen or bathroom can be deceiving. Remember that before the fittings were plumbed in, these rooms were probably not very different from others in the house. Windows and fittings can be simply altered so that the rooms can be turned into bedrooms or rooms for any other purpose.

Decide exactly how you'd like the rooms altered to suit your lifestyle and then consult a builder or architect on the cost of the work involved. There are nearly always one or two viable alternatives if the first estimates appear too expensive. Many builders can be slightly reticent about the probability of a scheme which looks over complicated, and may charge you more to cover any future possible mistakes of theirs. Therefore get two or three quotes, for your own peace of mind, and if possible on paper, including a penalty clause to cover time losses (which will nearly always mean more expense for the householder).

As it is difficult to pinpoint each item when rebuilding a large house or even just decorating a small one, there will always be a 'grey area' where the householder thinks he has paid for certain items and the building firm says he has not, as they weren't included in the discussion at the beginning, or written down in the original estimate. Make sure that you don't make this mistake by covering as much as you possibly can. Don't gloss over relatively minor points, such as skirtings, light fittings or paintwork. Carpentry is very labour intensive and costly, and the extras can add up to fifty per cent or more of the final bill if the standard of finish is higher than was first agreed between builder and client. Try to take the time to go over the estimates with your builder before he starts work. If you don't have the time then try to get help from someone who can 'break down' the building costs in detail.

Remember also that estimates are exactly that, *estimations* of how much the work will 'probably' cost. They are very rarely exact, so take this into account when you begin building work and allow a percentage over and above the original bill. The more thorough you are, the less likely you are to have problems over the final settlement with your builders.

KITCHENS
Positioning your kitchen correctly is probably the most important factor when rebuilding or when you are going to buy a new house that is in need of a fair amount of structural work.

ABOVE: This room was originally a bedroom which led through to a room beyond. Because of its position in the house, the bedroom had infinite possibilities, particularly as a kitchen. The alterations would have to be dramatic, as the low ceiling of the extension beyond blocked most of the light. Alluring glimpses of the garden beyond could be seen at the bottom of the extension through a small window, making it imperative that the new structure should not block the view or obscure the sense of light and space.

LEFT: The conservatory extension allows a great deal of light to filter through the suspended open shelving unit.

A badly sited kitchen can result in hours of extra work and much walking backwards and forwards from the eating area to the kitchen. If it is poorly lit through a lack of windows or dim lighting, it can be a very depressing place to have to spend a large part of your day in. Alternatively, the kitchen you've inherited with the house could be in the perfect position but badly laid out – the cooker may be built in an area without work surfaces, or the sink positioned so that it is impossible to stack dishes before or after washing them. Whatever the problem, consider moving the units around and adjusting the plumbing to suit. It could take very little replanning to have the kitchen you want and if you take into account the hours you spend in the kitchen it may be a worthwhile expense.

If you decide that the kitchen is in the wrong part of the house to suit your needs, and there is very little likelihood of your moving the units from one room to another, you will probably be able to design your new kitchen in a room not very unlike any other in the house. Kitchens and bathrooms are usually built in exactly the same way as the other rooms in the house but as soon as the fittings are plumbed in they take on a completely new look, almost defying change, as they appear so permanent. If you find you are standing in an empty room, without so much as a cooker point in sight, try not to be thrown for lack of inspiration. Start by positioning one unit and work around the kitchen from there. Alternatively, go and see one of the thousands of kitchen fitters and designers and ask them to plan a kitchen for you. Even if, in the end, you decide not to buy their units, the charge for the drawings is comparatively small and may save you many problems if you're designing a kitchen for the first time.

Repositioning your kitchen. If you decide to build your kitchen in a completely different room than the one in which it is plumbed, you may have to take into account some or all of these factors.
● Is there enough natural light and if not, does it really matter as the hours you spend in it may be mostly at night?
● Is the room large enough to accommodate all the fittings and units you need? Also, if it's short of

space, is it possible to maximize the space available, so that every corner or top shelf is of use and in easy reach?

● Consider the position in which you are about to rebuild it in relation to the dining room or another eating area. If it is far away from the dining room, is there enough room in it for a table so that occasionally you can avoid the trek backwards and forwards and therefore have some of your meals in the kitchen?

● Could the room next to the kitchen be of use as a dining room or have dual purpose so that if the room you designate as the kitchen is too small, some meals could be eaten in the room next door?

● If the room you choose as the kitchen is too small, could the area outside be built on to so that the kitchen is made larger or a breakfast room/playroom added, so making the kitchen one enormous family room?

This last suggestion may be the most successful idea to follow up of all of the above, especially if you are short of space and have the room to build on to. The addition of another room close to the kitchen can be a real bonus in houses which are short of space on the ground floor and for families with small children, as it is possible to be near them without actually falling over them while you are cooking.

When you extend the kitchen area, remember that the new extension may take away some of the light from the kitchen. Take into account all of the alternative positions of windows or skylights. Consider replacing or fitting glass roofs and removing obstructing walls so that both rooms retain as much natural light as possible.

W.C.s

How often has it crossed your mind that your bathroom is at the wrong end of the house, or that is is in some other extremely inconvenient position? Your WC may be far too many stairs above the living room or kitchen where you spend your days with your children.

Houses that were built many years ago were designed for other lifestyles and many were designed without bathrooms or WCs. These were added in the last century and were often plumbed into the most suitable room in the house at that time.

LEFT: By adding a glass conservatory extension the problems of light were overcome. This open shelving divides the kitchen from the adjoining dining area, and filters light into the room at all times of the day. The area next to the shelving is used as a breakfast area, with a large family table, a neat bench seating unit and enough room for a pretty wooden display cabinet for china.

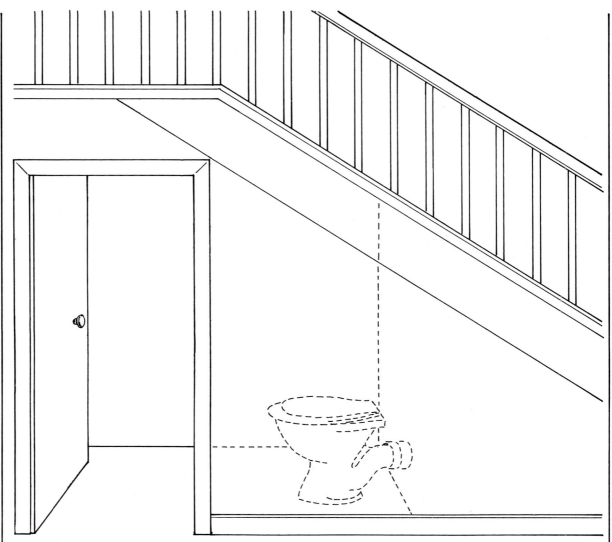

ABOVE: A newly converted coat closet.

If you live in a house that has the space or building permission to extend the property, such problems can be relatively easily solved, by adding a WC or a bathroom next to a bedroom or on the ground floor.

Problems arise in terraced houses or in those which have no room to build on and those without planning permission, even though they have the space. In such cases you may have to allocate areas within the existing property. One of the perfect places to build a WC is in a house that has an understairs recess (perhaps including a hallway that is large enough to accommodate a WC as well as a doorway down to the cellar). If your house has no cellar then the whole area could be used for the WC. This idea may seem improbable until you think that the area needed for a WC can be less than one square metre.

A hallway will also serve as a natural lobby for a WC. The drawing on page 20 shows how the understairs cupboard was converted into a perfectly adequate WC even though the width of the cupboard was only 80cm and the length 120cm. Although it is possible to convert very small cupboards and recesses for a WC as the area needed is so small, the cost of the plumbing may be prohibitive if the new drainage positions are too complicated. Also there are health regulations concerning the height and fall of the soil pipe. One of the more simple positions for a WC is on an outside wall, where there tend to be fewer problems with drainage as there is usually enough of a 'fall'. Consult your builder about costs versus position and work from there.

It is sometimes easier to build a partition in an existing room and to create a new room out of the old. If you can position the new room so that the doorway opens into yet another room or into a hallway, the telephone box effect will be lessened, as the structure in the room in which the WC has been partitioned off can be disguised by adding bookshelves or cupboards to the sides of the partition. Eventually, with the additions of other features such as cornices, the new structure will be hardly noticible.

It can be very difficult for you to envisage major changes such as these when you stand in the room that you would like to rebuild, as the solid appearance of the walls belies change. Remember that partitions can be simply made. Wooden frames with plasterboard attached can easily be put up and easily taken down. The whole process of partitioning off a room is much more simple than most people realize.

The most complicated part of the exercise may be deciding *exactly* where you want the new WC, taking into account the fall of the drainage and the cost of the plumbing! It may help to draw a precise plan of the ground floor and look carefully at the layout before you decide exactly where you want to put the new WC.

Lastly, remember that plumbing work can be cheaper than decorative work and unless you meet major structural problems, the pipework could be adjusted with a minimum of expense. Once again get a number of quotes from different builders and as much helpful and sensible advice as possible.

OPPOSITE: A bathroom *en suite* was created out of an area on another floor, on the half landing, by knocking through to the bedroom and building a small staircase down. The staircase was supported beneath the steps although it would have been possible to have fitted a small iron spiral staircase which would have needed no extra support.

BATHROOMS

In larger houses it has become almost commonplace to find that there is an *en suite* bathroom adjoining the master bedroom. The trend for more bathrooms per household is rising steadily. More and more boxrooms and small bedrooms are being converted to bathrooms, so much so that it is unusual to find recently converted or modernized four or five bedroom houses with fewer than two bathrooms per household and perhaps one other included in the master suite.

If you have a spare bedroom or small room next to the master bedroom, adding a bathroom may be just a simple process of knocking through the connecting door and plumbing in accordingly.

If however you have no extra room, you may have to 'steal' the space you need by planning the new bathroom so that you take a small area of one room and some of another. Sometimes this can work perfectly as the new bathroom can serve two bedrooms with as little as a square metre lost off the area of each bedroom. A new bathroom can be constructed out of a bedroom and a study in a similar manner. The new bathroom solved many problems as the only other bathroom was on a different floor. If the wall between the room is not a load-bearing wall, you will have few problems with the partition work. If it is a load-bearing wall, you will have to support the area above with an RSJ (rolled steel joist). Once again, the drainage plays an important part in the decision on position for the bath, sink and WC. You may have to 'juggle' the positions of the new plumbing around so that you meet all the requirements of the District Health Authorities, but the extra expenses incurred, if there *are* problems, are usually outweighed by the advantages of having an extra bathroom.

The landing area in your house can often be brought into use if you are looking for more space. The area next to the bedroom in the photograph on page 94 has been used as a sort of library area, though the total size in fact is well over the required amount for a bathroom (usually two and a half square metres is adequate) if the shelving was removed, allowing room for a passageway as well. A doorway could be added, built into the hallway rather than the bedroom, and another door built on to the landing, so that the

bathroom and bedroom would have a small lobby or passageway.

You may find that there is absolutely no extra room in the areas in which you would like to build a bathroom. Perhaps you should consider a small shower room instead, maybe built into the corner of one of the bedrooms. Pumps can be fitted so that the shower can be built in any

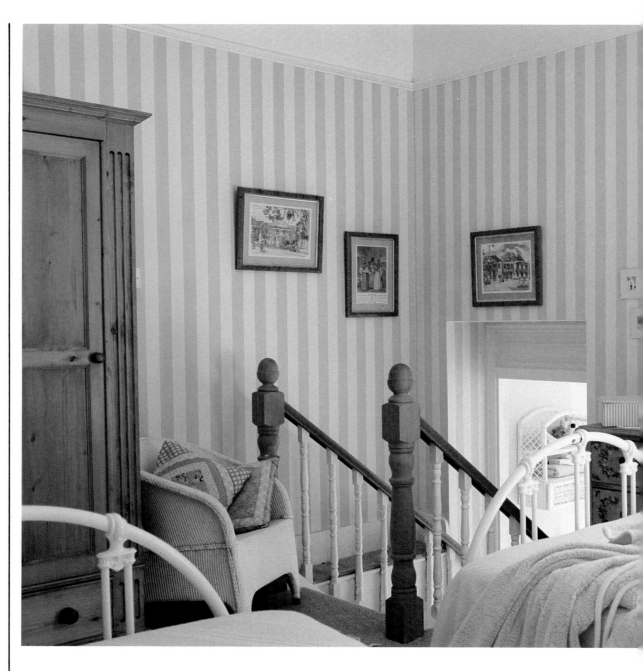

position in the house. A shower needs a very little space and often quite basic plumbing works (as well as being much more economical than a bath). As mentioned before, the areas to the sides of the structure could be filled in with cupboards or shelves so that the shower looks like a natural part of the room.

If you are not short of space, with many bedrooms or boxrooms that could be changed into a new bathroom, you can consider making your bathroom and bedroom into a complete

bedroom, dressing room and bathroom *en suite,* or building cupboards between the two rooms or two sections of one room so that one area serves as a dressing room and one as a bathroom. To be able to bathe and dress in one area alone is not only a great luxury but can also be a good selling point later on. In such cases the master bedroom need not be that much bigger than the bathroom, and you could fit cupboards into dressing rooms rather than in the bedroom.

CHAPTER 2

EXTENSIONS

EXTENSIONS

PREVIOUS PAGE: This extension was created because of lack of ground floor space. The house originally ended by the picture next to the plant. The new structure, with windows all around, allows sunshine in at all times of the day.

The rugs help to break up the large expanse of wooden floor, creating an atmosphere of warmth and comfort. Pale colours open up the area further, well placed furniture adding to the illusion of spaciousness. Often, one large picture is enough for a room, especially if the image or colours are strong enough within the picture.

As lifestyles change, so do our living requirements. Nowadays we spend more time eating, playing and living in the same rooms as our children, and therefore we need larger rooms.

There is often a lack of space on the ground floor. Young children need their own areas in which to play freely, away from the kitchen area, but perhaps within earshot or sight. This can be almost impossible in houses that were built over a century ago as there are very few that were built with a play area on the ground floor.

Apart from the needs of families with young children, ground floor space has become an important consideration when weighing up whether to buy a property or not.

If you have the space to build an extension, this could be the answer to your problems. There are several ways to utilize the area you are about to build on to its fullest. One of the methods you can use to solve the problem of a shortage of rooms both upstairs and down is to build an extension so that two rooms are formed, one up and one down. The room upstairs could be connected to the first floor of the house, perhaps creating another bedroom, a small study or even another bathroom, while the downstairs extension could form a new kitchen, dining room or playroom.

There are many houses with no shortage of ground floor space, but a lack of extra bedrooms. Perhaps the answer in this case would be to build a garage annexe, so that the additional bedrooms would be on the same floor as existing ones and with easy access to bathrooms. The area below could be used as a garage or storeroom.

There are many alternative ways of adding extra rooms to your property, so consider all of the different possibilities before making a decision, weighing up how each one could improve the layout of the house.

The idea of building an extension, as a solution to a lack of space in your house, can sometimes be overlooked as the price of the building works can be exhorbitant. However, the cost of moving house can also be prohibitive and often there is very little wrong with the old house other than a shortage of space. It is very easy to become attached to an area, you may find you need to be in reach of the local school or your job. Think carefully about how the house you live in could

be improved or enlarged to suit your needs before you consider moving on.

You need to weigh up the financial advantages or disadvantages involved in adding on to the property. You may feel you are over-investing in the building. (This, perhaps, is a slightly less common consideration than others as there are relatively few occasions when a well built addition to a property which is short of space becomes a devaluing factor or handicap when trying to sell the property at a later date.)

It is however worth bearing in mind that building works on this scale are expensive and time-consuming. The importance of allowing enough light into a new extension cannot be over stressed as generally any extension that is not almost completely glazed, will block some light from the room it is added on to. You can help to counteract this by adding extra windows to the room beyond the extension or by glazing as large a percentage of the extension itself as is possible. Skylights can be also used to help provide extra light where the extension is built on only one floor level.

ABOVE: The finished conservatory extension (see p.15) allows a spacious seating area, an informal eating area and a light and airy kitchen.

Fully glazing the roof of the extension may be the perfect answer for very dark rooms. The first section of the conservatory on page 18 is more of an extension than a true conservatory as both sides of the extension are brick built. The only glazed sections are the roof and the front end, which let in a maximum amount of light to the room beyond which is used as the kitchen.

In another typical case, a family with very little space in which the children could play added a playroom and a conservatory extension. This was particularly useful when they needed to entertain informally as there was very little room at the existing kitchen table. The conservatory/extension became a breakfast room in the morning, a playroom during the day and a beautiful second dining room at night.

A large skylight was built into the side of the extension that overlooked the kitchen, so that the kitchen lost very little natural light. The conservatory area, which led off the dining room, was glazed so that the light in the area beyond was unobstructed. The final building was as beautiful as it was practical, solving the family's problems of living space perfectly.

CONSERVATORIES

A cheaper or more practical alternative to a brick built or solid extension is a glass conservatory. Now that double glazing has become almost a standard feature in most conservatories, they are being used as extensions to the house, rather than as winter plant sanctuaries. A conservatory built as an extension in this way has become a valuable addition to a house with a lack of space.

Conservatories block very little light to the rooms beyond because of the large percentage of glass used in their construction. They are extremely attractive garden rooms – a comfortable way to enjoy the outdoors without experiencing any of the discomforts! If you wish to use your conservatory throughout the year, you need to build one that is draught-proof and adequately heated and ventilated. The panes will need to be double glazed, and the whole structure protected against the weather by adequate sealing measures and painted in tough weatherproof paints.

There are many firms today involved in the building of conservatories. More and more people are beginning to realize not only what an

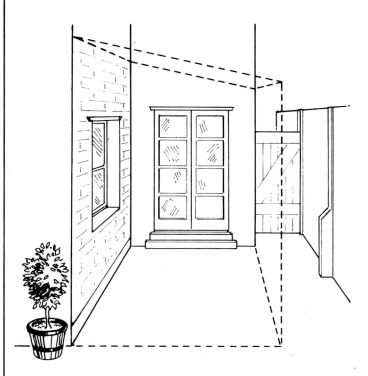

LEFT: The total area in square metres to the side of this semi detached house was large enough to incorporate a small conservatory.

attractive addition they make to the house but also how pleasant it is to be in a room with an unobstructed view of the garden, protected from bad weather without feeling completely shut in.

In the drawing of the conservatory above you can see how the sides of the house were neatly used to form half of the structure. The conservatory was used to fill an area between the dining room and the kitchen. It became a natural play area for the children as it could be watched over from both rooms. It is fully double glazed and well ventilated. Its heating system is unconnected to the existing central heating system so that it can be adjusted as necessary or turned off completely if the room is not being used.

The simplicity of its decor is the key to a well designed conservatory. The garden beyond serves as decoration, and so there is very little need for colour or pattern in a room from which you can see a riot of colours in the garden. Let the flowers and plants beyond the conservatory add colour to the room and then add your own plants inside the conservatory, keeping decor to a minimum. The shapes and colours of the plants will provide interest and patterns within the conservatory.

31

CHAPTER 3

COLOUR

PREVIOUS PAGE: This room is painted in very soft colours. The wood of the picture frames, the skylight and the small cupboards contrast well with the creamy wall colour. The area above the daybeds is limited by the sloping ceiling, yet the close positioning of the shelves and the pictures is interesting and attractive but not at all cluttered, because the tones in the room are neutral. There is a little else to focus on except the ornaments and pictures.

The daybeds are built so that they serve as storage units, the tops are hinged so that they can be used to store bed linen or duvets, perhaps the perfect answer for bedsits or studio flats.

This chapter could be extremely short or volumes long. The scope for using colour in interior decorating is endless. It is the key to successful decoration: beautiful and expensive furnishings can be wasted without a sympathetic background, and the most stunning furniture can go unseen in a room decorated in a style which competes with it.

With a basic knowledge of colours and their co-ordination, you should find that decorating your house is a simple and delightful task rather than a daunting one.

Everyone has a particular sense of colour and style, especially when choosing clothes. Perhaps the most difficult transition is from choosing the colours for your clothing to choosing the colours in paints and fabrics to decorate your house, as the amount of colour or pattern spread over your walls is obviously going to be that much more dramatic, through its sheer quantity. The concept of mixing and blending colours to suit holds true for both ideas. The most beautifully dressed people are those who use the colour of their clothes as a foil for their looks, just as the most attractive rooms are those whose furnishings blend well with the colours of the walls or stand out against them, complimenting and contrasting with each other.

As many people use their pictures or furniture to provide the colour and design in their rooms, the tendency to choose pale shades as a background for wall colours is universal. Pale colours reflect light well, making rooms appear spacious, and so they are used regularly for decorating walls and ceilings. A white or cream wall can be as dramatic as a brightly coloured or patterned wall. One well positioned picture or ornament against a white wall will create all the drama or emphasis needed in an otherwise simply furnished room.

The photograph on page 1 shows how well this Mediterranean style of whitewashed decoration works. The overall effect, although bare, is warm and delightfully simple without being too blank, the warmth of one object or picture deeply emphasized by a stark background.

As a contrast, the photograph on page 36 shows how deep colours can also be striking in their simplicity. The solid deep red colours of the walls are not overpowering even though they are broken only by the pictures on the walls and the ornaments in the room. The room is welcoming and cosy, the strength of colour a pleasure, rather than a disturbance.

There are far too many unwritten rules about the use of colour: lemon and green can appear sickly, bright red is rather harsh and so on. All of these may appear true if used without care or thought but none are true when used in context in a well designed room. Example after example can be found of colours used in strength or in odd contexts and yet they work extremely well.

The photograph on page 90 shows just how well a mass of blue with touches of other primary colours works. Children love bright colours and the colours used in their rooms should reflect this.

Use colour to create warmth where there is little and to make rooms appear restful where life can be over stressful. Colour can completely change the mood of your room. It is the simplest and easiest way to transform one room into another.

PAINT FINISHES

There has been a lot of interest recently in specialized paint finishes. There are now many books on ragging, dragging, stippling and numerous other finishes. Each of these techniques gives a very individual finish, not only for walls, ceilings, fireplaces and staircases, but perhaps most usefully on old and ugly furniture, which can be given a new lease of life.

Very few of these techniques require a great deal of knowledge or technical ability, just an interest in the subject and a small amount of practice. The finished effect can be as subtle or as strong as you like. These finishes are meant to give your room that individual look, a look no-one else can match exactly as the work is done by hand. Difficulties usually arise only when you attempt something on a large scale that you haven't mastered on a smaller one.

Some of the most attractive and professional looking techniques are those done with very subtle colour changes, between two or three colours. Try using a painted cream base, a beige stipple on top of that and yet another colour, ochre, ragged on top of the beige. Other combinations could include a pink painted base,

ABOVE AND OPPOSITE: This room had a large window so that it was full of light. It was, however, intended to be a study and painted in colours that were deep and striking, so in some ways in this room the light was not fully used.

This perhaps should be taken into account if your rooms are dark and there is little you can do or wish to do. Emphasizing the lack of light by painting them in dark colours can make your rooms cosy and welcoming.

The recesses to either side of the fireplace have had shelves and cupboards fitted so that a television and video could be hidden from view.

terracotta ragging over the pink and a sponged peach colour on top of the pink and terracotta.

If you find that you have mastered the subtler colour changes then try the more dramatic ones. As you can imagine, mistakes will show up much more easily between black and white, navy blue and cream and so on. Tread with caution and practise each effect before you start on the walls or on a piece of furniture.

Keep the medium (the glaze or paint) reasonably thin so that it glides on relatively easily, and follow the instructions carefully, especially those on tins of varnish and glazes as some do not mix together and others don't 'take' on top of each other. Read as much as you can about these paint finishes, and always practise first on a small area, either on lining paper or on a bit of furniture that won't show until you feel confident enough to start.

ABOVE: The ceiling in this room was very high, making the room seem unwelcomingly tall and cold. The window also added to this impression as it was too high. The area beyond the window was to be turned into a verandah (see page 6) so that the windows were replaced with double doors opening onto the verandah.

A very awkwardly shaped recess in the chimney breast also had to be altered as the shape was rather coffin-like.

OPPOSITE: The tented ceiling not only lowers the height of the room but adds colour and drama echoed in the colours chosen throughout the room. The border, at picture rail level, also helps draw attention from the high ceilings. The coffin-like recess is now completely altered by the addition of shelves and colourful boxes of toys.

Primary colours add a sense of fun and excitement to a room. Touches of red and yellow in an otherwise colourless room will impart a feeling of warmth. Painted boxes and furniture serve as marvellous and colourful storage units for toys.

Don't be afraid to try unusual colour combinations and techniques, there are so many new and beautiful effects which you'll only discover if you attempt to mix patterns and colours.

Remember also that there are three basic or primary colours, red, blue and yellow. All other colours (except for black and white which can't be classed as 'colour') are mixed from these three colours. You therefore need very little in the way of painting materials to achieve very varied finishes. Household materials – sponges, rags, brushes etc. – will provide the basis for many techniques.

The finishes on the next few pages were all achieved very simply, and relatively inexpensively, with very exclusive looking results, which can be easily copied and adapted to suit the colour schemes in your rooms.

If your ability as a decorator or designer really does not stretch to painting the walls yourself, employ others to do it using your ideas, or as a last resort buy wallpaper with similar paint effects. The variety of wallpapers with painted effects is enormous and although not as individual as those done by hand, these are certainly just as attractive if chosen with care.

OPPOSITE: The paint finish in this room is a combination of stippled and ragged colours. The base coat is an ivory or cream coloured eggshell and terracotta and eggshell blue paint are alternatively stippled and ragged on top. The effect is subtle, but helps the colours in the material for the curtains and chairs link together with the carpet.

Strong colours, or heavy furniture can sometimes provide a solid background for pale fabrics or walls.

LEFT: The softly sponged colours in this very male dressing room echo the colours of the curtain, seen in the mirror. They co-ordinate with the master bedroom on page 79, a range of bruised purples and browns and a creamy base.

Sponged and stippled paint finishes are just some of the techniques in a range of finishes that can add an individual and unusual look to your walls. They allow you to incorporate many colours in the room, pulling the whole concept together in rooms where previously few colours linked together.

WALLPAPER

Wallpaper is the perfect answer for disguising a bumpy wall or creating a pattern on the empty walls of a large room. It is also a way of adding period elegance and style to a room full of antique furniture. There are many styles, patterns and designs to choose from, so many in fact, that the choice can be bewildering. Start by deciding on exactly what pattern or colour you're looking for and work from there. For example, if your rooms are large but dark, choose a paper that is light in colour, although clearly or strongly patterned, so that the strength of the pattern fills the room and the feeling of dim and empty spaces is lessened.

Smaller patterns or close 'prints', are not as 'filling' or as dramatic, as they give an illusion of space that a bolder pattern will not.

Stripes are particularly useful when you want to give an impression of height or formality: the bolder the stripe, the stronger the illusion. One of the most stunning places to use a striped wallpaper is in a hallway and stairs. The stripes

ABOVE AND RIGHT: This attractive attic
room was full of unusual ceiling shapes and
heights. The striped wallpaper helps to
emphasize height as well as enhancing the
sloping ceilings.

Strong tones like the black furniture add
depth to the room. Touches of pink in the
cushions and pot plants supply warmth and
life to an otherwise soberly coloured room.

emphasize the height between the floors, making a feature of the stairway.

Use pale and softly patterned wallpapers in rooms that you want to appear spacious and light. Soft colours are an excellent foil for dark wooden furniture, such as mahogany, oak and teak. The colours and shapes of the furniture stand out starkly against a cream or white background. Neat floral styles or regular printed wallpapers, and those with small geometric patterns are some-times most attractive in bold or deep colours. For example, deep red paper with small cream spots hung in either a dining room or a study, creates a wonderfully cosy atmosphere, yet emphasizes a traditionally masculine type of decor. Grey or donkey grey with a small pattern is also very elegant in these rooms as the wallpaper serves as a perfect background for etchings or prints.

Brightly patterned wallpapers are perhaps the most exciting of all as they add light and warmth to the room. However, it is as easy to tire of a beautiful but highly patterned wallpaper as it is easy to tire of strongly patterned clothing – perhaps even more so as there is so much more wallpaper in view! Tread carefully when choosing papers that are intended to decorate your house for a number of years.

One of the simplest ways to 'finish' off a wallpapered room is by adding a border, either above or below a picture rail or a dado rail. It is easy to imagine how striking a contrasting border would look on a matching wallpaper with either a strong stripe or print.

Borders often bring the colours together in the room, perhaps by matching the carpet to the wallpaper or just by echoing the colour of the upholstery in a favourite piece of furniture.

Borders do not always have to be flowery or thin. Some are modern and eyecatching, others, especially childrens nursery borders, can be up to one metre deep. In some rooms, the border may be the only form of decoration: the walls simply painted and then the rest of the colours in the room highlighted in the border (as on page 74). Here the shower and bath are totally shaped and disguised by the border which runs from the shower to the bath and beyond. The colours in the room are all echoed in the flowers in the border which provided the basis of the decor for the room.

CHAPTER 4

FABRIC

FABRIC

PREVIOUS PAGE: One of the most unusual ways to divide a room, but perhaps the least harsh, is to use a swatch of fabric to curtain off one side from the other. Here a plain fabric, linked in colour with the curtains at the far end, provides a subtle yet distinctive divide between the sitting and dining areas of the room.

Very little expense has been incurred, yet maximum effect has been achieved. Once again, the touches of colour in the furniture, pictures and ornaments are enough decoration in an otherwise simple but cosy room.

Curtains and other materials play a very important part in making a room feel comfortable. Apart from keeping out the draughts and insulating the room when drawn, the fall of the material gives an impression of cosiness that cannot be created by other decorative treatments. Curtain pelmets and swags, or the style in which you drape your curtains will lend an impressive and immediate sense of style to your room.

Use large swatches of material in rooms when you wish to give an impression of grandeur or luxury. The bigger the sweep or fall of the material, the greater the effect.

When you decide on the fabric for the room, let the pattern dictate to an extent the style in which you hang it. If the pattern is most attractive at the hem of the curtain, or at the base of the length of material, hang the curtain so that it shows this to its best advantage. Try a Roman, festoon, or Austrian blind so that the most attractive parts can be seen at eye level.

If there is no strong pattern but the material can be draped extremely well, you could arrange the pelmet in swags and tails, pinning back the curtain also very extravagantly with large tie-backs.

Use the pattern in the curtain in conjunction with the colours and shapes of the room. Many people start decorating a room with a particular piece of material that they like, choosing the colours of the paint for the walls or wallpaper from the colours in the material. (This could also include the choice of carpets and cushions.) It is a good idea to start decorating, first of all choosing the fabric in this way, rather than the opposite way round, as it will be hard to find a piece of material that has the green of the carpet, the yellow of a favourite chair, and the blues of your old china collection.

If you find that your rooms are a wonderful mixture of odd sofas and chairs in assorted patterns, you could 'pull' the whole room together by choosing one colour from the existing materials in the room and emphasizing that colour. Make the borders on the curtain or on the wallpaper blue, the larger of the cushions on the sofa blue and then pipe the lampshades in blue. A theme like this, running through a mix-and-match room, can give the room a sense of well-thought-out design.

BELOW: This dining room was subjected to the 'white-washing' method of decorating as it was so difficult to imagine the finished look. Floor to ceiling front curtains (PREVIOUS PAGE) give the room a sense of grandeur and formality. The patterned blind adds touches of colour and creates a cubby hole effect. The room is large enough to accommodate the very heavy mahogany furniture (OPPOSITE).

Fabric can also be the interior decorator's answer to spartan rooms. If you're short of furniture or personal effects and wish to make your room look cosy and welcoming, you can immediately transform it, introducing pattern and colour by draping rugs over chairs or hanging them on the walls. You can carry this idea further by using materials for table cloth covers, and by using very full and intricately draped curtains and pelmets to decorate the windows. Perhaps the last idea is the most popular decorative ruse, as a window that is draped in beautiful curtains becomes a stage that catches your eye as soon as you enter the room.

One of the most unusual yet attractive ways to handle curtain treatments and introduce more fabric into the room is to curtain off part of the room instead of using a rigid screen or a more solid divide. Your room takes on an intriguing tent-like effect, the softness of the material implying comfort and warmth. Screen off part of your room by building a simple structure of three frames and hinging them together as in the drawing. Cover with fabric and suddenly you'll find that your room seems smaller and cosier.

Another unusual and inexpensive way to make use of fabric is to make a false ceiling of material in a room with awkward proportions or where the ceiling is in a poor state of repair. The former often occurs in bathrooms and WCs of old houses, perhaps because a large room has been partitioned off to make the bathroom or WC. The material may need to be joined and then tacked to the walls or on to batons, the edges hidden by glueing piping into place. You can fold the fabric in lines or draw it together in a spiral toward the centre, so the fabric radiates outwards. It could also be draped softly over a centre baton like a circus tent. Any of these methods will make an ordinary room seem very special.

RIGHT: A mass of untidy items can be hidden in a recess behind a clever curtain treatment.

OPPOSITE: The colour of these curtains echoes the colour of the room, so they continue the colour, line and space. The striped borders of the curtains match the painted panels on the walls.

If you're short of cupboard space, consider screening off a corner of the room by hanging fabric as a screen, either creating a shelf system behind with boxes or putting up a hanging rail instead. If you use a fabric that co-ordinates with the material already in the room you will find that the material cupboard blends in well and becomes an acceptable part of the room, perhaps even a feature.

The same idea can be used as a way of hiding contents beneath or on shelves, another inexpensive storage system. This could also be adapted for a window seat, with cushions above; not only would this look attractive, but would be extremely practical as extra storage space.

Washbasins can also be covered from below in the same way, so forming a basic cupboard. The basin has 'velcro' stuck to it which keeps the material in place. As the material can be removed, it can be washed or replaced when necessary.

There are also many unusual methods for hanging curtains without using standard curtain rails. Some of the loveliest curtains are just

OPPOSITE: This curtain treatment is not only
light and pretty but can give complete
screening when the sides of the curtain that
are hooked back are allowed to fall together.
Very little daylight is blocked from the room,
yet complete privacy is maintained.

looped over a pole, hanging down loosely at night and pulled softly to one side during the day. This can look very simple and attractive, especially if there are two windows side by side, as the two curtains pulled back in this way look very theatrical.

Draped front curtains with lighter curtains behind (as shown in the photograph on page 51) also give an impression of a stage even though the curtain behind is drawn up in a more regular fashion. A pole could be used to make your curtains look fuller and more traditional by stitching closely to the pole (as the drawing shows) so that the material is heavily rushed when it is hung. Tie the material away from the window during the day and let it fall together when you want the curtains drawn.

If you are short of fabric, or are unable to fit the curtains so that they hang to the floor, or just prefer them to stop at the sills, there are some interesting methods you can use. If you have a run of windows such as a bay window, you could fit screens so they could be removed during daylight hours and easily put up at night. Most windows have recesses the screens could be fitted into, the catches holding them in place. The finished effect is stunning it its simplicity. Beautifully patterned fabric can be shown off at its best as there are no folds to hide the patterns. The material is easily stapled around the frame, which is simply made by using four batons or lengths of wood held together with metal struts or brackets in each corner. The fabric structures are light and can be quickly put up and taken down.

Roman blinds also show fabrics to their best, especially when they are 'drawn' as they too lie flat when they are hung. The borders or pattern on the blind can be sewn together so that you can still see them clearly when they are drawn up (see page 49).

Festoons or Austrians give a fuller or more luxurious impression than Roman blinds, as they are gathered extensively but they show very little of the design of the fabric. They often look best of all when used with plain fabrics as the combination of pattern and 'swag' can be overpoweringly feminine. Austrian blinds can be slightly less rushed so that the effect is a cross between Roman and Austrian, not completely flat but not over drawn so that the folds drape softly from

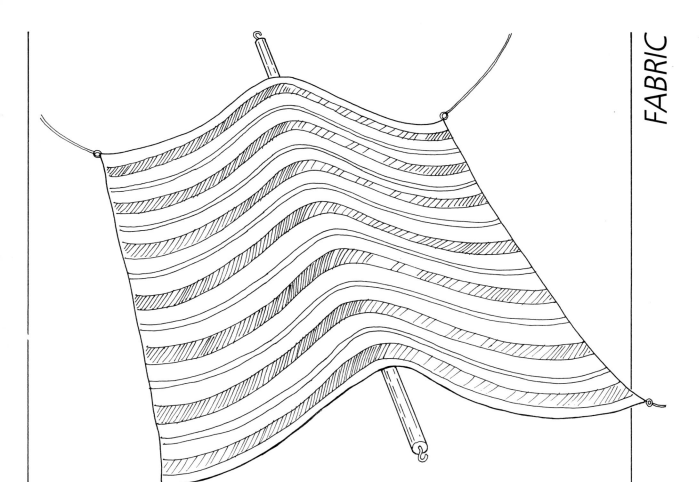

one side of the curtain to the other.

Fabric roller blinds come in kits that are available from many shops, so that you can choose the material you want to match your colour schemes, and then stiffen the fabric yourself with special sprays or fixers to produce your own blind.

Whatever curtain treatment you choose, use fabric as a way to decorate your room, creating warmth or style. If your windows are huge and imposing, emphasize this by choosing curtains which highlight their size or underline the grandeur. If they are surrounded by a decorative framework, think of a way of screening them without hiding the frames.

Until your curtains or blinds are fitted, a room can seem uncomfortably open or unwelcoming, but you will be surprised at how this feeling is dispelled as soon as they are hung.

OPPOSITE, ABOVE: The understairs area lends itself to many treatments. In this case the area has become a study, though it could equally have been a cosy snuggery or cloakroom.

OPPOSITE, BELOW: It is easy to make your own unusual form of net screening. Keep the form of screening as simple as possible.

ABOVE: Cover bumpy and unsightly ceilings with simple tenting pinned, stapled or hooked up and supported by a central pole.

CHAPTER 5

LIGHT

ABOVE: Even though the staircase and top landing are undecorated, it is possible to see how much light is being let into the hallway from the skylight behind. A second skylight, out of sight, was added later and in the photograph opposite you can see how much extra light you can gain from such an addition.

Replacing a dado rail has returned a sense of proportion to the walls so that the stairs and hallway appear less tall and narrow.

PREVIOUS PAGE: Shutters or louvred doors make wonderful screens, allowing in maximum light whilst giving added security. This window is next to a roof terrace, not only a problem for privacy but also for security. Louvres can be fitted to open many different ways. The louvred window at the top has been propped on to a pole so that the effect is slightly tropical in design.

As was mentioned in earlier chapters, the importance of natural daylight or a good lighting system cannot be overstressed. A room that lacks light is immediately restricted to certain uses. If you are planning to rebuild or attempt major building changes you may have to consider altering the window positions or adding others if you think there might be too little daylight in the room.

Although there are many complex and extensive lighting systems on the market, nothing is as effective as natural sunlight, so make sure that this is taken into account when designing a new property or altering an old one. Consider all of the options. Skylights can be used in the centre sections of the house. This is a marvellous way of letting in light to old houses where previously there was very little, especially on staircases which are generally dark areas. It is possible to have skylights fitted in most roofs. However, if you are in the process of re-roofing, you have even greater scope for changing the style or size of the skylights as you may be able to incorporate quite a large glazed panel in the roof instead of the more regular size. Most houses are restricted, to a certain extent, to light from one direction or another, as very few have windows built on every side so that there are times when some rooms are filled with light and others on the opposite side of the house are much darker. A new skylight could let in light at all times, so that morning light and afternoon light is practically unrestricted to all areas.

Building or replacing skylights may not be the only method of allowing more light into your hallway. Glazed panels in and above your front door will make an enormous difference too. If you are worried about the security risk that glass doors may pose, instead of a more solid barrier, you could use a decorative grille to cover the glazed area for extra security. There are many types of coloured and decorative glass on the market, some can be etched to your own designs and give quite adequate screening whilst allowing in a maximum of light.

If you would rather have a more solid door, consider having a panel of glass above and at the sides of the door surrounding the frame. The side panels could be built so that they were narrow enough so as not to present a security risk. The panel above the door could be made a little

larger, and perhaps both could be covered by a grille. There is no doubt that some of the above methods are worth considering as a glass fronted door is often the only source of light in the hallway.

At the back of the house, the same method could be used to allow more light into the back passage or hallway. The French doors on page 64 are in keeping with the style of the house and also allow a maximum amount of light into the passageway.

The windows in the room on page 38 were replaced with French doors so that there could be access to the verandah from the playroom. The playroom has been made darker as the verandah roof shades some light from the room. However, an extra window was put in on the other side of the room to compensate for the lack of light.

RIGHT: The skylight in this room faces south, even on the dullest days this room appears full of light although there are no other windows. This room was to be made into a bathroom although it was only two metres square.

OPPOSITE: The soft greys echo a feeling of space and light: the colours in the room are restful yet elegant. Keep colour to a minimum if you wish your rooms to appear spacious.

RIGHT, ABOVE AND BELOW: The back door was originally half the size of these French doors. The bottom half, solid wood, only the top panel glazed. Even though the hall is still undecorated in these photographs, it is possible to see how opening up a doorway provides light and a welcome view through to the garden.

OPPOSITE: The finished hallway, painted in colours which make the most of the light. The floor is covered in a hard-wearing lino, as the door leads out to the garden.

The effect of being able to see through, from front to back of the house opens up the hallway and allows the light to reach parts that were originally shut off, appearing dark and cramped. Hallways are notoriously difficult to light. If you can solve this with extra windows or doorways, you can make the whole house appear lighter.

ABOVE: The stained glass windows in the hallway could hardly be seen from the outside as they were surrounded by dark and peeling paint. Inside, however, the paintwork was light and the patterns showed up clearly with the sunlight behind the door.

OPPOSITE: Very little was done to the hall, so as not to detract from the windows.

The floor, which had lost many tiles, had to be covered with new flooring. Lino was chosen as it is a warm covering but reflects the traditional style of the old floor.

Even on dull days the light reflected through the glass throws patterns on to the walls and the floor and lights up a substantial part of the hallway and stairs.

LIGHTING

Hallways and landings are often poorly lit with natural light as they tend to be built towards the centre of the house. You can improve the amount of daylight that is let into a hallway by incorporating a skylight, but if this is impossible you may need to consider using other methods. Wall lights are often used to light up passageways, as they do not take up floor space which can be somewhat limited in a hallway. They are perhaps the most attractive form of lighting for a passageway, stairs and landing as centre lights are difficult to screen from above or below. When you walk up or down a staircase you are often able to see the naked bulb of a hanging light on another landing. There are shades for wall lights which direct light either upwards or downwards depending on which area you wish to be lit most directly. The mural painted above the wall lights (seen on page 68) makes the wall lamps look as attractive during the day, when the lights are not in use, as when they are turned on at night.

Pictures could be hung above a wall light so that the light could be directed toward them in this way. If they are framed in glass, check that this is non-reflective to avoid shadows on the glass obscuring the view of the picture.

Wall lights give off an even light at an almost perfect height as they can be fixed to the wall at eye level. There are many fittings and styles to choose from, though there is often a maximum wattage for the bulbs so that you may need several lamps of a similar style to achieve the required amount of light.

Spotlights. Spotlights have now become so well designed and are made and fitted in so many different styles that the scope for using them is endless. Whilst recessed spotlights are almost totally unobtrusive, they tend to give out less light than those which protrude or those which are attached to a ceiling strip or runner.

Spotlights are probably used at their best when a particular part of the room or picture needs to be highlighted. They may be very useful, especially for the latter reason, as large pictures are particularly badly lit by picture lights which are often attached to the frame or the wall above the frame and the pool of light they cast downwards is often too small an area to cover a large picture.

ABOVE: This wall light has had a mural of a spray of flowers painted behind it. When it is lit, it throws an arc of light on to the flowers so that it is not only functional, but extremely picturesque.

Lighting alone can decorate your room, shadows cast interesting pictures and make cosy corners. Highlight pictures and ornaments to create the right atmosphere.

RIGHT: This dining room has been decorated in very soft beiges and browns so that the white table mats and silver cutlery stand out starkly against the dark furniture. Using light and dark in this way can replace the need for colour in a room designed to appear dramatic.

The standard lamp echoes the traditional atmosphere and casts a mantle of light at the perfect height for intimate dining.

A full run of spotlights, evenly spaced and angled in different positions, will give a room almost perfect light without the harsher effects of fluorescent lighting.

Striplighting or Fluorescent Lighting. These are probably the most 'complete' lighting systems. They are often used as 'office lights' and are perhaps slightly harsh for uses in the home except in the kitchen. They can be fitted with high wattage bulbs, and are used as ceiling lights in areas where there is little natural sunlight.

Centre Lights. Generally these lights cast the least attractive form of lighting of all. They neither give sufficient light for reading, nor do they create an atmosphere of cosiness or warmth, as the light is too diffused and not low enough. They are best used for areas where there is no need for 'character' lighthing or little space for table or wall lights, such as utility rooms or pantries, where the walls are highly shelved or space is somewhat limited.

Standard Lamps and Table Lamps. These lights are probably the best form of lighting with which to create an intimate setting. Standard lamps will, in addition, give adequate light for reading. Angle poised lamps, which can be as tall as the more old fashioned standard lamp, are probably best of all, for strong lighting with which to read.

Table lamps cast a low and dimmer pool of light than most other lamps, and are therefore often used in sitting rooms and bedrooms where stronger lighting is not usually necessary.

The lights you use can enhance or destroy the atmosphere you are trying to create. If you want your rooms to appear intimate and cosy, keep lighting to a minimum using table lamps and wall lights. If you want your room to appear striking or dramatic, a well positioned spotlight or two will do just that. The shadows cast by the carefully angled lamp create a strong image. An even more cheerful scene can be set up by using brighter lights – by using several spotlights together, or a run of wall lights, or one or two fluorescent lights.

Selecting your lighting should take you some careful thought as the work which goes into decorating the rest of the room could be nullified with the use of incorrect lighting which does not echo the mood of the room. Remember, too, that at night a couple of well placed lamps can disguise a multitude of sins.

Window Screening without Loss of Light. Protecting your privacy without losing too much light from the room takes a certain amount of skill if it is done subtly and without drawing too much attention to the choice of screen. There are many alternatives to net curtaining but perhaps none as effective because of the sheer simplicity of nets. They are easily made and simply hung and there are many styles and patterns to choose from.

If you dislike the more regular form of hanging rail or wire, you might consider using a rod or wire at both the top and bottom ends of the curtains so that the fabric is stretched taut across the window (like mesh screening) rather than gathered together. A more permanent solution, but similar idea, would be to tack or staple the nets straight on to the window frames or on to a

ABOVE: Table lamps are good mood setters and also the best lights to read by.

69

ABOVE: Use mirrors to reflect light where areas of your house are shut off from direct light. The small window on the landing below allows enough light in to be reflected up the next stairway by the large mirror on the landing.

Not only do mirrors work as light reflectors, but they also double the space they reflect so that this landing appears most grand.

baton frame which could also be removed if it itself is held up with clips or screws.

The effect of nets used in this way is reminiscent of homes in tropical countries where screening like this is used to repel insects as well as to protect privacy.

Other methods of screening your windows

70

with fabric could include using a very thin muslin or other similar fabric held across the window halfway up, saloon style. This type of curtain looks particularly attractive on brass rods. It suits sashed windows extremely well as there is a natural 'break' where the bottom of one window starts and the other begins.

One of the best ways to screen your windows without the use of fabric is to apply the treatment to the glass itself. There is a plastic cling-film-like material that can be stuck to the panels of glass, making the glass appear tinted and oblique from outside so that it is difficult to see in. However, very little light is changed inside and the difference in the glass barely noticeable.

If you are involved in major building changes to your windows, you may consider replacing the existing panes of glass with others that have a similar system 'built in'. The glass itself is tinted so that the view in is obscured from the outside and yet the view is unchanged from the inside. Sometimes it is possible to 'mirror' the outside of the glass completely and still retain a normal view through the inside.

Other ideas include using heavily frosted glass on all or just the lower panes or choosing from a selection of coloured or obscured glass to create a pattern for those of your windows that are overlooked.

There are companies which specialize in period glass who will design and match patterns to the existing patterns of your house. Equally, you could commission a stained glass panel to screen your room from passers by, gaining a picture and achieving total privacy.

In the photograph on page 58 the shutters were used as much as for their design as for the extra security they gave the room. The room is right next to a roof terrace which could have posed a security problem.

Fixed louvred doors or shutters do not allow in as much light as other forms of window screening, but they are extremely attractive as well as very good at forming a basis for extra security. They are perhaps best used across windows where they can be opened or shut depending on the amount of light needed.

Shutters with slats which open or close are perhaps the perfect solution to window screening with style.

ABOVE: One of the many ways to screen a room overlooked by the street is to use a half blind of material or of solid wood.

CHAPTER 6

LARGE AND SMALL ROOMS

RIGHT: This photograph shows only a third of an enormous bathroom. The scope for change seemed limitless here. There was enough room to incorporate a shower, WC, built-in bath, dressing table unit and a wall of cupboards. Juggling all of these things together so that the bathroom worked efficiently was perhaps slightly more complex than normal, as there were so many factors to take into account.

As the bathroom had so many cupboards and units to be built in, the pipework could be hidden behind the new structures, so very little was piped below the floorboards. A useful tip to remember if your floors are solid or if you are unable to pipe below.

PREVIOUS PAGE: In small bedrooms it is worth taking the time to find pictures of furniture which fit the shape of the room. The area between the curtains and the wall to the left of the bed is only just big enough for a child's bed. The area is made even cosier by painted ribbons and balloons and with a small bedside table. Furniture that echoes the shape and style of a room goes a long way toward making the room feel comfortable and well adjusted. Over sized chairs and tables can make an average sized room appear much smaller.

You may wish either to emphasize or to disguise the size of your rooms. A large room can be daunting and unwelcoming unless carefully furnished; whilst entertaining in a small room can become claustrophobic.

Emphasizing or featuring the shape or size of the room is usually a more successful approach than trying to disguise its size, as not only is disguise a complicated and sometimes costly business, but if your room is barn-like it may always appear so, however dimly lit and cosily furnished. Similarly, if your room is little larger than a cupboard it may always appear so even with the help of clever paint effects and white walls. You may not improve the illusion of space that much, whatever you do.

Decide on how effectively the disguise will work for your rooms, accept the limitations of the rooms, yet try to look for opportunities the room presents in other ways. Explore the possibilities of removing cupboards and incorporating nooks and crannies in the room, either for seating or for storage and so on. If your rooms really are ridiculously small or very large and there is little you can do to change this, then feature their sizes. Go to great lengths to make the best of that room. Eccentricities are always interesting and rooms that are out of the norm can be a delight if they are designed and decorated with style, flair and the best made of the unusual aspects of the room.

FEATURING THE SMALLNESS OR DISGUISING THE SIZE

If your rooms are tiny and you feel there is little you can do to improve the feeling of space, you could take the opposite tack and revel in the lack of space and its tininess. Create a delightful den-like room, one that is full of character and warmth.

One of the simplest ways to create this atmosphere is to pattern heavily the walls or colour them deeply. The addition of many pictures or prints will emphasize this feeling of busyness in the room. Hang pictures as low as possible or at eye level which will also help to underline the feeling of intimacy.

Using decorative wallpaper and a matching border at picture rail and dado levels will help to lower the ceiling height, making the room appear cosier and smaller. Carry the line of the borders around doorways and windows, emphasizing

ABOVE: Because this bathroom is so large it also serves as a dressing room. This was taken into account when choosing the colours for the room. The varying shades of soft mauves were picked out from colours in the border.

The cupboards and the bath structure were painted in the same colours so that they blended into the overall picture. As there were so many built-in units they would have stood out starkly against the background if they had been painted white.

Housing the WC tank not only reduces refilling noise but also provides a useful shelf for books or ornaments.

their shapes and creating interest in the unusual angles.

If you wish to lower the ceiling further consider tenting the ceiling with fabric. The chapter on fabric discusses this in more detail.

You can make your room appear smaller by using an abundance of furnishings and ornaments, which could cover your table tops and shelves with little space from one are to another.

Arrangements of flowers and plants fill awkward corners, the general feeling of a 'full' and lived in room is easily achieved with plants. These are not only attractive, but also create a feeling of life and growth which is why conservatories and rooms that are full of plants are so pleasant to sit in.

Use rugs spread over the floor or carpets to 'break up' large areas of similarly coloured flooring. Mix patterns and styles of fabric – your room will still appear well designed or thought out if you have a basic colour or two that you work around.

All of these ideas help to reduce the feeling of space or emphasize the smallness of the room. You can do so even further by 'losing' part of the room by screening off an area. You can do this with floor screens or by curtaining off one end of the room. As the picture on page 46 shows, the curtain effect is extremely graceful as well as practical, easily assembled and economic. In that picture the curtain was used as a room divider rather than as a screen, but the idea would work equally as well for screening one end of the room.

Remember also that colour can play a great part in disguise. Keep the colours strong in a room which you want to appear cosy. If you want to have walls which are painted rather than wallpapered, consider using deep colours with paint effects such as ragging, dragging, or sponging. Red paints that are used in this way and are then lacquered are wonderfully warm and inviting colours.

Try to steer away from using pastels or light colours as they reflect light well and will make the room appear bigger rather than smaller.

As mentioned earlier strong patterns in the fabrics used in the curtains or on the sofa, cushions and chairs help to underline a 'busy' image. You can co-ordinate different patterns by

OPPOSITE: This small washroom was created out of a part of a hallway on the ground floor. The design of the room centred around an old discarded draining board.

In small rooms it is essential to have good storage if you intend to use the room regularly. The ground floor in this room measures less than two square metres yet the room has adequate space to work in as there are enough cupboards to hold cleaning equipment.

Classic uncluttered lines, like the plain blind and the brass taps, emphasize the feeling of a stark and functional room yet the warmth of the wood adds a touch of homeliness.

ABOVE: The whitewashing method of imagining all the walls white and the room empty of furniture had to be used to realise the full potential of this room.

OPPOSITE: Making the most of a large room often means taking the time to work out how best your furniture and fabrics will compliment the size of your room. The four poster bed fills this room without swamping it because not only are the ceilings high enough to accommodate it, but the drapes for the bed blend into the colours of the wall. The posts of the four poster emphasize the height of the room as do the full length curtains, both work together to compliment and balance each other.

emphasizing one colour on the piping of the cushions, the tie backs in the curtains, on one or two cushions and the colours of the rugs or carpets. In this way the room will 'pull together' and yet look wonderfully unrestrained and 'naturally' decorated.

If you have a room which is uncomfortably large, you may have to consider separating it into two areas and dealing with each end individually. In this way both ends can be given a more intimate setting just by enclosing that feeling of too much space. Do this by building an arch, so that the rooms are not completely separated but the divide is just hinted at. The arch could be brick built or shaped with fabric if the effect was to be less permanent. The two 'rooms' could be painted very different colours or wallpapered at one end and not at the other to emphasize the

ABOVE: A large room can be divided by well placed furniture.

different ends of the room.

If this idea would be too dramatic a change in a room which had furniture or curtains which matched at both ends, perhaps the paint changes on the walls of both rooms should be more subtle – from beige to cream or oatmeal to ochre.

You could also position your furniture to form a natural divide, each end turned inward creating a separate area. Use shelves to fill bare areas in rooms which are uncomfortably large. Careful use of pictures and prints will disguise much of the sensation of empty space.

Try not to leave large areas of flooring without either a rug or a piece of furniture. Large and empty floor spaces give the impression of galleries or hallways, an image you are trying to avoid.

If you panel the room either with batons pinned to the walls or with painted squares, you will help to 'break up' walls. The areas within the panels could be painted different colours from

ABOVE: One well placed screen can divide one large room into two smaller ones.

the outside area. Panelled walls also give the impression of formality as they are often found in the drawing rooms of ancestral homes.

If you are short of pictures, try not to spread them around to cover impossibly large walls. There is nothing worse than one small picture sitting high up on a practically empty wall, emphasizing the fact that there is little else to help cover the space. Group pictures together on one wall and try to use different treatments on the others.

Finally, remember that clever lighting can conceal large areas of the room that you wish to 'lose'. Don't use overhead lights if you can avoid them as they dispel any feeling of intimacy. Keep lighting to wall lights and table lamps if possible (except where you wish to emphasize or light up one particular area). The use of a spotlight will be particularly helpful at times like this for concentrating attention on one area rather than a more

ABOVE: One well placed screen can divide one large room into two smaller ones.

general light which underlines a feeling of space.

FEATURING THE LARGENESS OR EMPHASIZING THE SIZE

To make a room appear bigger than it is, you will need to emphasize the space within it. This can be done by spacing furniture cleverly and by sympathetic colour treatments.

To make a room appear larger is made harder if the room has a severely low ceiling, or awkward corners that completely cut off one end from another. However, you will often be able to take attention away from these problems by emphasizing other points about the room which help to underline rather than detract from the feeling of space.

If your ceiling is very low, try not to focus attention on it by hanging anything, including light fittings, from it. The more blank you leave an area, especially if an area nearby is filled with items that attract your attention, the more that area fades into obscurity. Paint low ceilings white or soft pastel colours so that they reflect light and fade away rather than sitting closely above the head.

Use furniture and screens to hide obscurely shaped corners or to create interesting areas or shapes on the opposite side of the rooms. Sometimes a balancing effect like this works to even out an area that was originally awkwardly arranged.

Try not to arrange furniture so that your path through the room is obstructed, which immediately stresses the shortage of space that you are trying to disguise.

Allow the furniture to follow the lines of the walls so that the 'movement' is underlined. This may sound somewhat unusual but you may only make a room look more awkward by placing a square piece of furniture in a rounded wall space. A corner cupboard will fit naturally into a corner, and so on.

Try to keep the furniture in proportion to the room. Emphasize the length of long walls with a long sofa or table. Keep lines 'clean' – avoid placing pieces of furniture across the room which break up larger areas into smaller ones.

If you have two rooms which have been knocked into one but neither end seems to link with the other, paint both ends the same colours so that the feeling of continuation is unbroken, and place furniture so that both ends link together, either by facing pieces toward each other or by using a table or sofa as a link between both rooms.

Furniture should always be placed so that there is easy access, as mentioned earlier. If you obstruct passage through a room with badly placed furniture, you will destroy the feeling of spaciousness.

Carefully selecting and placing ornaments so that they too appear to have a certain amount of space around them will help to dispel a sense of clutter.

One well placed picture will convey a feeling of style and design that several badly hung pictures will not. Pictures can be used to create interest in areas that were once pitifully bare.

When you decide on how you'd like to decorate your windows, keep in mind that elegantly hung, full length curtains go a long way toward creating a sense of grandeur that small rooms generally lack.

Try to keep curtain lengths as long as possible in rooms where you want to emphasize height and space. Curtains which end at the window sill will have the opposite effect.

Colour and pattern can play a great part in detracting attention from size. By using a pattern or colour that is echoed in all parts of the room, the feeling of continuation is again reinforced. Plain and 'cool' coloured fabrics perhaps work best of all here as they fade into the general scheme rather than demanding attention.

Rooms that are decorated in monotone can be stunning, and the lack of colour will help to dispel any cramped sensation. You can create all the interest you need to by using the shapes of the furniture and the ornaments and pictures to provide colour and pattern within the room. The careful positioning of well chosen plants will enhance the effect you have achieved.

Once again your lighting will either detract or add to the mood you've created. Don't over light the room to underline the feeling of space, but make sure that no area is neglected or left in shadow. A mixture of wall lights and table lamps will cast separate pools of light on different areas, the feeling of space within the room underlined yet again.

CHAPTER 7

STORAGE

PREVIOUS PAGE: The area below a bed is often wasted space. Although there are many new storage systems for underneath beds, these cupboards are one of the most attractive. The bed is an average sized double bed and is almost a metre high, so the storage space below is substantial. The open shelving could be used to house many things – including a television for early morning viewing!

The screen is no more than a painted trellis but it gives the bed a feeling of extra privacy, the plant adding a slightly exotic touch.

BELOW: Window seats are attractive and useful, providing extra storage and filling awkward areas.

OPPOSITE: Shelving systems do not have to be boring or traditional. This is based on a ladder idea so that the contents are easily available whilst providing decorative storage.

Those of us with squirrel like tendencies and a natural inclination to store our possessions in every available nook and cranny know that there are many unusual and inexpensive ways to store things without giving over large areas to extensive and expensive built-in cupboards. The following are only some of the many storage ideas you can incorporate in your house.

Firstly, consider whether or not built-in cupboards are the answer to your storage problems. Although they are expensive, they are often well worth the money spent on them, as they definitely add to the value of the property, especially if they are well built and attractively designed. There are many styles and layouts, but if you intend to have a whole wall covered in cupboards, it might be best to break them up with areas of open shelving or perhaps with a seating area. Unless it is in a large room, the new structure can be overpowering.

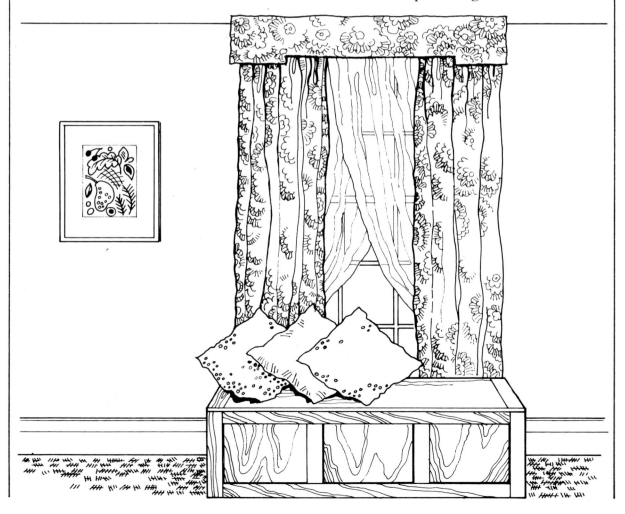

ABOVE: This room was to be both a guest room and a workroom. Although it was little used as a guest bedroom, changing it from one to another would have meant rearranging the room each time a visitor arrived.

RIGHT: The problem was solved by building a large cupboard over a metre deep, so that it could house a desk and shelves. The doors shut the desk away if necessary, so that work can be left untouched.

The recess would have proved an awkward area to fit other furniture in, so the cupboard desk idea worked perfectly and solved both problems.

ABOVE: This picture of the children's room before the bunks were built show perfectly how angled and yet interesting the ceiling shapes were. Children love awkward corners and small boxes.

RIGHT: The large bookshelf between the beds is like a walk-in cupboard making both sides of the room seem cosy and yet still connected. Children's storage need only consist of painted boxes or baskets, the more extraordinary the piece the more they seem to like it.

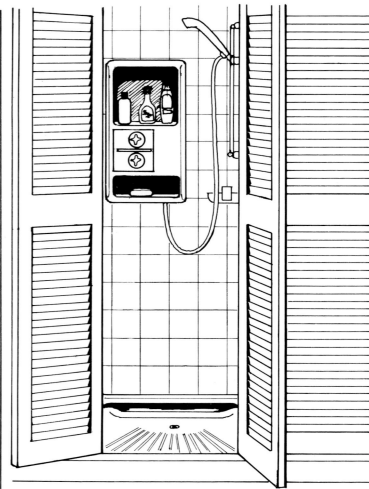

If your cupboards seem to tower over the room, this may be because they are painted a different colour to the rest of the room. If you have wallpapered the room, use the panelled area of the cupboard to infill with matching wallpaper. If there are no panels or the room is just painted then match the colour of the room to the paintwork of the cupboards. By blending the cupboards into the room in this way, you will find that they seem much less overpowering. A continuous border around the room and across the top of a wall of cupboards will also help.

When designing the cupboards think of all the ways you could disguise the great wall of doors that built-in cupboards generally have. Shelves and doorways help to open up the spaces between one area and another as seen on page 88. These methods are perhaps particularly necessary in small rooms as the ability to see the wall behind the cupboards brings back a sense of depth to the room.

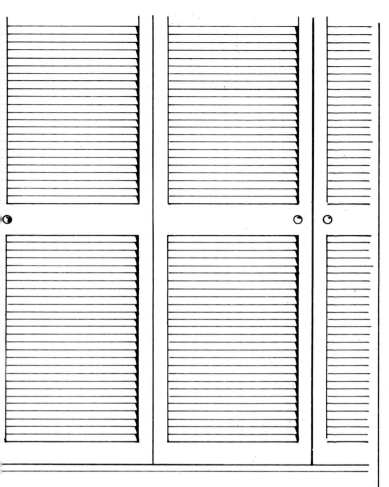

LEFT: You can incorporate a totally disguised shower unit in a dual purpose room with louvred doors to the cupboards.

If your rooms serve dual purposes – a play-room during the day and a dining room at night, for example, or a study until overnight visitors arrive – then your built-in cupboards could serve as complete room storage systems. In the photograph on page 88 the cupboards are over a metre deep and house a desk and chair and enough shelving for the owner/artist to shut away the lot at night without disturbing her work or having to move too many items from one place to another.

If your budget will not stretch to complete units like these, you will have to decide exactly which other systems will suit your needs and your finances. There are simple shelf systems which can be put together relatively quickly and there are also systems that can be bought ready made. In the chapter on fabric there is a section which covers using fabric as door fronts. This can look very attractive if the fabric matches or contrasts well with the existing fabric in the room. During the day, or when the shelves are

ABOVE: Landings are often too narrow to furnish properly or seem too large and draughty.

OPPOSITE: The bookshelves run from floor to ceiling along one wall, giving a library effect to the area. There is just enough room for a window seat chair and table, but a little room has almost been developed.

being used, the fabric can be pinned or tied back like small curtains. A mass of toys or other objects can be neatly hidden in a system like this yet easily reached when necessary. The drawing on page 52 shows how simply you can make this fabric fronted shelf system.

Playrooms for children are great rooms for

ABOVE: Tea chests can be stacked and
bolted together for toys.

which to invent unusual storage systems. As well as the many boxes and chests you can buy for them, crates and tea chests can be painted different colours and stacked and bolted together as in the drawing opposite. They could also be lined with assorted fabrics making wonderful cubby holes for small children as well as practical and economical storage systems.

Flat lidded baskets not only provide simple storage (as they can be stacked one on top of the other) but are very pretty and look charming in bedrooms or even kitchens where they can store a variety of implements. Handled baskets can be hung from the ceiling or cupboards.

Beds are wonderful places to store things under if they are raised on legs or if they are built so that there is space for a cupboard or drawers below. The photograph on page 84 shows a room with a cupboard built under the bed. The cupboards are two metres long and one metre wide, an enormous and unusual storage area. More traditional beds tend to have unused areas beneath them, and there are many underbed 'suitcases' which could be used to utilize this space.

Perhaps the most satisfying forms of storage are the repainted or refurbished boxes, chests and old containers that are given a new lease of life. They not only give you an enormous amount of satisfaction, creating something new from something old, but also may save you a lot of money as new furniture can be extremely costly.

One of the first mistakes made when you move into a new home is to try immediately to change the whole style of furnishings in the house to your own, tearing down cupboards which 'offend' and throwing out outdated furniture, little realizing that under several coats of old green paint may be a beautifully grained piece of wooden furniture. We are often confused by the door furniture on a piece, more often than not the only indication of period. Cupboards have stayed similar shapes for decades, as have chests of drawers, but it is the 'offending' handles and door trims that are the indicators of style or taste. These can be removed with a minimum of effort, and most holes easily covered with a new handle or with the appropriate filler. With a coat or two of paint and some new handles, the new piece of furniture created will fit into the style and design of your home.

CHAPTER 8

AWKWARD
SPACES

PREVIOUS PAGE: Sometimes small and awkward spaces can work in your favour. They offer natural recesses to frame your furniture and belongings.

This child's reading corner is inviting and colourful: the smallness of the area is underlined by the small chair and bookcase. Colour can highlight or disguise a difficult space – use it as a method of creating interest in an otherwise dull or awkward space.

OPPOSITE: This small dressing table and stool fit neatly into the area between the chimney breast and wall. The little chest of drawers just fits into the recess in the chimney breast.

Often it takes time and thought to find the right piece of furniture for a difficult space, but it is worth doing.

Most houses contain areas which are awkward to fill, either too small for a chair or chest, or too narrow for a bed. Such areas can be the most interesting parts of a room, especially if their unusual shapes are well highlighted, rather than half-heartedly disguised.

There are so many different niches and corners in every house that it would be difficult to cover even half of the problems they cause. However, look at the area and try to imagine what piece of furniture or object would look best within it. Use the area as a frame, spotlighting the piece inside the niche. Consider buying a perfectly shaped plant and highlighting it with spotlights: the effect is stunning, especially if the plant is unusual or perhaps tropical. In the photograph on page 105 the window ledge was built in this way because the area was originally a chimney breast. As chimney breasts in older houses are usually a main part of a supporting outside wall, the area above the window was reinforced and the main structure left intact. The window was built into the chimney breast and a very wide ledge was then left in front of the window. The area was used decoratively, the flowers creating a marvellous focal point for the room.

Most houses that were built over 30 years ago were built with fireplaces. The fireplaces of yesterday are often left unused or are bricked up. There are many ways to use your fireplace so that it is not only useful but also a feature within the room.

You could fill the area with shelves and use it as a small niche for books or ornaments. It would also look attractive if you used glazed doors to protect the contents.

If the fireplace is high enough it can be the perfect spot to hide a television, as generally the layout of the doorways and windows of the room will enable the occupants to group chairs or tables around the fireplace. In a dining room or kitchen the fireplace could be filled with wine racks – an easily accessible cellar.

Chimney breasts also create awkward spaces to either side of the fireplace, especially in rooms that are short of wall space. One of the ways to solve this problem is to use the area for purpose-built cupboards or shelving. Often the area is too big or too small for a piece of furniture but you could make it into a 'folly' by emphasizing its

ABOVE, AND OPPOSITE: Although it is hard to tell from the picture, the walls and ceiling of this room slope in three different directions and are very low in places. This room was to become a children's bathroom, so it was possible to put a large bath under the eaves as the ceiling in the foreground above the bath rises more steeply, allowing you to stand upright in some places. The sinks were built at a slightly lower height than normal, so that the room has taken on a charming 'bathroom in wonderland' atmosphere.

RIGHT: Small niches or cupboards can be used purely for decorative purposes in an otherwise plain room.

OPPOSITE: When this room was converted into a kitchen, a window had to be added, which was placed inside the chimney breast. The resulting windowsill was very wide as the chimney breast was almost a metre deep. To make a feature of the area, it was filled with baskets of dried flowers and attractive ornaments. In this way the light was not obscured but the view of a very ugly wall outside was partially disguised.

shape, perhaps with curtains, and highlighting the recess with spotlights.

One of the classic awkward spaces in a house is the area under a staircase. Without doubt most areas like these are overcrowded and often ignored as attractive features. If your understairs cupboard is going to remain as a cupboard, use as much of the area as possible by shelving the walls fully and having hooks in all other useful areas. If the area is superfluous, consider removing any existing cupboards and using the area as a decorative point. The niche-like area could house a seat and library-like shelves on one or both sides, making a wonderful snuggery, or it could be built so that open shelves displayed a collection of china and so on.

Highlighting an area with an attractive piece of furniture will also attract attention and is perfectly demonstrated on page 101. The dressing table is placed so that the corner of the room enfolds the piece, making the area seem secluded and welcoming.

Sometimes a wall in a long or thin room, can seem awkward, as can a low ceiling in a cottage. Firstly disguise the problem as well as you can by either breaking up the long wall or by making a low ceiling seem higher by distracting attention away from it. Then go even further by making sure that the more attractive points about the room are underlined with correct and sympathetic treatments.

CHAPTER 9

FINISHING TOUCHES

PREVIOUS PAGE: Use one or no colour at all as a background to highlight your favourite objects. Wood contrasts stunningly with white paint or tiles. The jugs and baskets are in keeping with the rustic basket of fruit, but the sink is very modern. The absence of strong colour allows each object to stand out clearly against the white.

OPPOSITE: Keep to one theme throughout a room. The small Victorian pictures reflected in the mirror are perfect period pieces for the pitcher and bowl and the bedstead. Pieces of furniture should harmonize with this theme, so decorate old furniture to take on a new lease of life and blend well into your theme.

To be able to say when a room is 'finished' is the hardest task a decorator has to face. Perhaps one of the best ways to tackle this dilemma is to look at the room and try to 'balance' the weight of the furnishings, ornaments, pictures and background against each other. This may sound more complicated or confusing than it really is. Your furniture may be modern – the lines simple, devoid of tassels and frills. The background and artefacts surrounding such furniture should reflect this, echoing shape and style with strong lighting and simple flower or plant arrangements. Too much clutter on table tops will perhaps over balance or undermine the effect you are trying to create.

On the other hand your furniture may be antique, your pictures heavily and decoratively framed and your materials strongly patterned. A room decorated in this way will be perfectly balanced and kept in period style with the addition of rugs, ornaments, flower arrangements and soft lighting.

ABOVE: Consider decorating your whole room around one favourite piece of furniture.

OPPOSITE: Pictures play a large part in decorating. Rooms without pictures are reminiscent of hotel foyers or other public places.
  There need not be a surfeit of pictures to provide an interesting view, but it is important to hang whatever you have to its best advantage. Pictures should not be just decorative props, but also central objects around which to design a room.
  The cottage wall in the picture is echoed in all the things that surround it – the colour of each piece highlighted in some way in the picture.

If you have a combination of both old and new furniture, as many people do, your task will be slightly harder although it may be more interesting. Here, the balancing act will take on new meaning as each piece will need to be positioned with careful thought, colours and shapes playing a much greater part than age or style. If you attempt to lump the whole lot together without giving each piece any thought, your room may look like a mixture of jumble. Just by moving one piece away from another by a metre or so or by allowing a certain amount of space between different period pieces you can create exactly the balance you are looking for.

Furniture has an odd knack of looking perfect in some spots and awkward in others, just as a piece of jewellery which should match one dress does not (even though it is a similar colour) yet the same piece will look wonderful with a completely different outfit.

Move the pieces of furniture about so that the height and shapes of each piece weigh against

RIGHT: It is possible to create a complete illusion with a mural. An extra window was painted on an adjacent wall to give the impression of a view through to a large garden and countryside beyond. The fabric above the picture was pinned on to a pelmet to make the mural seem more realistic.

OPPOSITE: The bedspread and painted cushions add the final touches of luxury to this dark wood bed, the wood showing starkly against the pale colours. Lamps and soft lights add a certain ambience to a bedroom.

The mural of a basket of flowers above the bed is enough decoration in an otherwise plain colour scheme.

each other. For some objects it is the colour that forms the link, for others it is the design.

Use your personal sense of design and style to arrange the mixture of old and new furniture in your house, staging each piece sympathetically, so that although it fits well into the entire scheme, it is given a certain amount of emphasis by itself.

The finishing touches you employ to decorate your home may not be as simple as furniture arranging or as complex as matching up each object in the room, from curtains to carpets, but if your room lacks a sense of co-ordination it may be that you have overlooked some of the basic touches that make a room seem lived in and attractively laid out.

You may have started with a general idea of how you wished the room to appear: chintzy and feminine, modern and relaxed, or excitingly colourful. You will need to follow these ideas through until the room has reached the stage where the furnishings and other objects compliment or contrast enough together, achieving your goal without going 'over the top'. It is knowing when to stop that clinches a beautifully decorated room.

If your furniture and furnishings do not match, or your new colour schemes do not hold together, then consider repainting the furniture and walls and recovering or curtaining windows or other pieces of furniture.

If you're unsure of where to start redecorating a room that is full of odds and ends, start by choosing a favourite piece of material, pick other colours from the pattern in the material, and decorate the room from there. If you own a beautiful piece of furniture perhaps you could use that piece as a guide to decorating the rest of the room, perhaps an old sofa with delicately patterned covers or a set of beautifully made curtains that are worth adapting to new windows. Collect odds and ends of material and drape them inside the room you wish to decorate. The larger the swatch of material, the easier it is to imagine the finished result.

Cushions, lamps, rugs and other bits and pieces will also make a great deal of difference to a room – they provide the warmth that hotels and other public places often lack. Don't be disheartened by the lack of character in a room that is newly refurbished – just one lamp, picture and

OPPOSITE: The panel is the base colour which links these objects together, being the background of part of the fabric, the picture and a cushion.

The painted lamp base is the delicate and clever method of linking fabric and lamp together. Attention to small detail such as this will make your room seem finished, whatever style you choose.

ornament will make the world of difference, making it truly your room.

If you have very little money to spend on decorating your house, but are a creative or capable do-it-yourself person, then you will be able to achieve many decorative effects by making them yourself without having to spend a lot of money. If, on the other hand, you have neither the money nor feel capable of making many of the items that adorn a well decorated home, do not despair, as a simply designed room can be as stunning as one covered with paint effects and dramatic curtaining. Weigh up your resources and your finances and decide on the most practical solution to both.

If you are short of finances to buy new furniture and curtains, consider using a spartan, modern style. Strong lighting, one painted table, a large plant and a comfortable sofa may be all you need. With the addition of a picture and perhaps one well placed ornament, the room will look positively stylish. If the colours are chosen with care, you can emphasize the spartan look. Rather than trying to disguise the lack of furniture, make a feature of the room's simplicity.

If your talents run to decorating walls with specialized paint effects, you may have a lot of scope when designing your home. There are many ways to decorate on a shoe string. Perhaps one of the best and most economical ways to redecorate in this way is to consider refurbishing any acceptable pieces of furniture so that they become an attractive part of the new scheme.

The following ideas are all used to give a room that 'finished' look. Each idea could be adapted slightly to suit other styles. There are no set rules about taste or design: your pieces of furniture and your ornaments will form the basis of your own finishing touches.

If you like highly decorated rooms, consider using a border to give the room that added 'finish'. This will not only distract attention from ceilings that are too high, but also from crooked or unlevel walls and oddly finished corners. In this way a border can also emphasize sloping ceilings in attic rooms by closely following the line of the ceiling. Borders also tie together the colours in wallpapered rooms, often forming a link between the colour of the wallpaper and other colours in the room.

ABOVE: Underline your style of decor by keeping pictures in context. Careful planning of furniture creates a strong sense of design in a room.

Hand-painted finishes such as ragging, dragging and stippling are the perfect answer to an individual look. As mentioned in the chapter on colour, no two rooms will look exactly alike as the effect is created by hand. The furniture in the room – the cupboards, doors and window frames for example – could also be matched with the same paint effects. You could 'go to town' on the different effects created within these finishes, filling gaps in the decor in an otherwise plainly furnished room.

Stencils also add a wonderfully creative hand finished touch to the room. They can match the colours of the room and also echo the shapes and patterns within the fabrics that are used for curtaining or for covering the furniture. There are methods of painting fabric with fabric dyes that are fully washable – these dyes could also be stencilled onto curtains.

Pictures, prints, posters or actual paintings are perhaps the most important pieces of all when considering whether a room is fully decorated or not. A room can be completely repainted, curtains hanging in place, photograph frames and other ornaments spread around, yet the room can still look bare and unlived in if it is without pictures. They focus interest perfectly. Use the colours or style of your pictures as a basis for decoration and you will be amazed at how the whole room seems to pull together. A very modern and strongly lit room full of angular steel furniture and decorated in monotone colours should not be hung with small flowery, old fashioned prints with pastel mounts and gilt frames for example. The frames and the pictures are neither echoed in the style of the design of the room, nor do they contrast well. One style is unsympathetic to the other, yet both could be equally attractive in the correct settings.

The use of fabric is very important in rooms you wish to appear warm or cosy. Rugs, curtains, cushions, screens and many other fabric covered items can take the edge off a starkly bare room and make it appear lived in.

Extremely feminine rooms are usually described as such because of the huge amounts of fabric and frills used to decorate such rooms. You can drape curtains or bedcovers so highly that there is very little need for other decorative items within the room. Curtain treatments will totally change the image of a room. Imagine your room with a plain louvred blind and then try to picture it with a set of swagged curtains, pelmets and tiebacks. This may help you decide on the image you eventually want.

As there are so many styles and patterns and coloured fabrics to choose from, use fabric to help synchronize a room that lacks a sense of purpose or pattern. With just one very abstract and highly coloured swatch of material, an otherwise ordinary room will be immediately transformed into one with style and character.

In most pictures of beautifully decorated

OPPOSITE: In 'finishing' your rooms, lighting will play a major role in setting the atmosphere. Clever use of lamps or concealed lighting will highlight all the things you wish to stress and disguise those you wish to hide. These candles seem to go well in this room because they are in keeping with the cathedral style window panes.

houses you will notice that there are nearly always bowls of flowers and dried flower arrangements or wonderfully ornate tropical plants. This is because plants are perhaps the key to making a room feel lived in. They add colour to rooms that are bare of colour. A room that has been decorated starkly with white walls and black or grey furniture, perhaps including steel rimmed pieces of furniture, and black and white photographs on the walls, will look absolutely stunning with one large tropical plant carefully positioned within it. The two styles – one so monochrome and harsh, the other so vigorously depicting life and growth – contrast strongly but perfectly.

Rooms that have been decorated with gentle and softly patterned fabrics and colours are again enhanced by arrangements of flowers that not only echo the colours within the room but also underline the softness of design.

This idea can also be employed in larger, less personal rooms. Hotel foyers are often full of flowers and plants which can introduce an atmosphere of relaxed comfort. Designers involved in decorating large public buildings know that the introduction of plants and flowers on a grand scale will transform these properties into places that appear more welcoming.

Remember that no two homes look alike, that your ornaments and pictures form the basis of your own style. Your home should be a reflection of your taste and sense of design. Allow this to develop by using your instinctive feeling for colour and style as a basis on which to start decorating.

Mistakes are seldom made if you spend a little time trying to connect one idea to another and linking all together in a general scheme. If you are nervous of taking on too large a project, build a design on one or two basic colours and work from there. You will slowly find that most colours and shades link or contrast well, as they do in the more natural world, outside the realms of interior decorating. Natural colours and patterns can be exotically stunning or breathtakingly simple. Most colours work well together if there is enough of a solid background to provide a 'rest': the dramatic colours of a bunch of assorted flowers is well set off against a background of deep green leaves for example.

CONCLUSION

CONCLUSION

PREVIOUS PAGE: Your house is a showpiece for future sale as well as a home for the present. Candlelight highlights the church-like windows of the conservatory.

RIGHT: Once you have created an unusual image, carry it through with matching furnishings and ornaments. Be adventurous with unusual ideas.

Your house or flat is today more than just a roof over your head. It can be one of the best financial investments you will ever make. Ensuring that your investment is well protected may mean that you will have to redecorate or at least maintain existing decor to an acceptable standard.

One of the most intriguing factors about the property market is the incredible variation of price between one property and another, although both properties may have been built in exactly the same style and in similar positions. The difference in price stems entirely from the way in which they've been decorated.

Making the most of your property, either by featuring eccentric or attractive qualities or by highlighting size and space can therefore not only be a creative exercise but also an extremely lucrative business.

Many people have noticed and have cashed in on the amount of money to be made from

interior decorating. Beautiful homes are not restricted to the rich or famous. Some of the most stunning homes are those that are simply decorated and painted in bold colours. Large or small, traditional or modern, your house should be considered as a valuable asset as well as a home. To ignore the potential your house has to offer is to limit the chances to maximize on your investment.

Design is so varied because taste is so personal. You can choose your style of decor from a massive and varied store of ideas around you. It is not the amount of money spent on the decor which ensures its attractiveness, it is the way it is put together.

Your decor may be no more than an image you have created, but if it is one that presents a picture then it may attract many prospective buyers in the future as well as providing you with a beautiful home for the present.

Acknowledgements

With love and grateful thanks to John, and to James and George, Katie McKie and Jillian Bennet, each of whom have suffered innumerable discomforts for the sake of new decorative ideas. Also, thanks to everyone who lent their support either emotionally or practically over the past couple of years and during the writing of this book.

A very special thank you to my editor Barbara Fuller for the hours of work involved in pulling the book together, and many, many thanks to Spike Powell for the trouble he went to over the photography. Thanks also go to John Grain the book's designer, and to Hilary Evans for the line illustrations.